Original title:
In Search of Purpose (and Coffee)

Copyright © 2025 Creative Arts Management OÜ
All rights reserved.

Author: Colin Leclair
ISBN HARDBACK: 978-1-80566-189-4
ISBN PAPERBACK: 978-1-80566-484-0

Every Drop a New Beginning

The kettle sings, a morning tune,
A dance with dreams, my coffee boon.
Espresso shots, a lively start,
Each sip ignites my sleepy heart.

With frothy clouds, my thoughts take flight,
Percolating plans from day to night.
Drip by drip, I chase the rays,
Savoring life in caffeine plays.

Quest for Clarity: A Caffeine Odyssey

Where's my mug? The quest begins,
A caffeine map to future wins.
Steaming lattes, brewed with cheer,
Adventure waits in each warm sphere.

I navigate through coffee lands,
With syrup rivers, sugar sands.
A cappuccino compass guides,
To deeper thoughts where joy resides.

Finding Flavor in the Everyday

Life's a brew of highs and lows,
In every cup, a tale that flows.
With every taste, a journey found,
In sips of joy, my heart unwound.

A sprinkle of laughter, a dash of fun,
Infused with dreams, this day's begun.
I savor moments, rich and bold,
Each mug a story waiting to be told.

Melodies of a Morning Ritual

Morning light, a symphony bright,
As coffee brews, I set my sight.
Mugs lined up like faithful friends,
In every drop, the laughter blends.

Stirring spoons make cheerful sound,
Each sip reveals the joy I've found.
With every pour, new tunes arise,
A caffeinated bliss in every guise.

Velvet Brews and Velvet Dreams

In the morning haze I roam,
Chasing coffee beans like foam.
Velvet cups promise my fate,
As I sip, procrastinate.

With each drip, a dream takes flight,
Caffeinated thoughts ignite.
Caramel swirls and frothy caps,
My mind weaves through hearty naps.

Infusions of Insight

A splash of cream, a hint of spice,
I ponder deep, though thinking twice.
Is caffeine wisdom in disguise?
Or just tricking my sleepy eyes?

Coffee beans, merry conspirators,
Stirring thoughts like whimsical narrators.
Every sip a riddle, a joke,
As I laugh at my tired yolk.

Intentional Infusions

In a mug shaped like a cat,
I brew intentions, imagine that!
Each press reveals a silly plot,
Overthinking? Nah, not a lot!

With each pour, my heart expands,
Unraveling life's nonsensical plans.
Espresso shots like quicksilver,
Tickling my brain, oh, what a sliver!

Drips of Destiny

As the kettle sings a steamy tune,
I muse about my fate by noon.
Coffee's magic, a liquid quest,
Makes me ponder, makes me jest.

The caffeine kicks, my thoughts disperse,
I chuckle at the universe.
With each drip, my fate's unclear,
But laughter's what I hold most dear.

Sips of Enlightenment

Each drop a thought, a little tease,
Awakening dreams with fragrant ease.
The mug a guide, with warmth and cheer,
Awareness grows with every sip here.

A swirl of beans, a laugh in tow,
Time slows down with a perfect flow.
The cup speaks truths, or so it seems,
Fueling the quest of silly dreams.

The Daily Brew

Mornings greet with a puff of steam,
Wake up, sleepyhead, chase that dream!
Pouring joy, one cup at a time,
Finding purpose with every climb.

Drips of wisdom, sugar and spice,
Life's little moments, oh so nice.
Sipping slowly, with a grin so wide,
Chasing the answers I always hide.

Navigating Flavors

Beans collide in a dance of fate,
A splash of fun, oh isn't it great?
The palate's journey, a wild ride,
With every taste, I laugh and glide.

Caramel hugs and chocolate dreams,
Every sip ignites our silly schemes.
I stir my thoughts, a whirlwind blend,
Who needs a map when I have this friend?

Lost in the Roast

In the steam I wander, so delightfully lost,
Mapping my life, soft flavors embossed.
Laughing at worries, they drain down the sink,
With every brew, I just think and think.

But wait! What's this? A new blend to try!
An adventure awaits as the beans sigh.
I stumble and giggle, but isn't it fun?
As long as to coffee, I stay always run!

Timeless Conversations in a Coffee Shop

Amid the steam and chatter loud,
I sipped my brew, feeling proud.
Topics ranged from dreams to socks,
Philosophers, they came in flocks.

A cup of mocha, my trusty guide,
Leads me through this morning tide.
With every sip, a joke unfolds,
The laughter is worth more than gold.

They pondered life, I slurped my cream,
While scone crumbs danced in our dream.
We laughed at fate, then brewed some fate,
Deciding on life's crazy plate.

So here we sit, a merry crew,
With coffee cups and dreams anew.
In every laugh, we seek a spark,
For joy's the light in this café dark.

The Blend of Life's Rich Flavors

Each morning sun, a cup in hand,
I stir my thoughts like grains of sand.
With laughter brewed and wisdom poured,
Life tastes better, can't be ignored.

A dash of cream, a sprinkle bright,
We sip on dreams, day turns to night.
Conversations bubble, frothy and free,
Finding fun in each caffeinated spree.

Espresso shots of chances bold,
Mugfuls of stories waiting to be told.
From barista banter to life's odd plot,
We mix the flavors, embrace the hot.

So raise your cup, let's share a grin,
As laughter dances, let the day begin.
In every sip, a tale unfolds,
Life's rich blend of flavors, for young and old.

The Pursuit of Balance

In the cupboard, beans sit tight,
Dreaming of a morning light.
Balancing dreams with caffeine spin,
Time for a sip, where do I begin?

Mugs stacked high on the counter's edge,
Coffee spills, a little pledge.
Find the joy in each warm sip,
With every cup, my worries slip.

Stirring chaos in a cup,
Feeling down? Just fill it up.
Laughing with caffeine's embrace,
Life's a race, but I've found my pace.

So here I stand, spoon in hand,
Navigating my dreamland.
Each brew a step, each sip a cheer,
In the game of life, coffee's my peer.

Whispers in the Steam

Steam rises like a morning song,
Each little bubble doesn't last long.
Whispers swirl in the kitchen air,
Awake, alive, without a care.

Mugs clank like a morning band,
Waking dreams at my command.
For every drip, a giggle spills,
In the ritual, find more thrills.

The kettle sings, a merry tune,
A playful dance that makes me swoon.
Beans grinding like a morning chat,
Lost in moments, imagine that.

With each swirl, purpose found,
In every sip, new joys abound.
So here's to mornings with a gleam,
Finding magic in the steam.

The Power of a Pour

With a pour, a new day starts,
Liquid magic warms our hearts.
From the pot, life's liquid gold,
Moments brewing, stories told.

A drip, a drop, then a rush,
In my cup, a vibrant hush.
Filling spirits with that first taste,
In this adventure, let's not waste.

Watch it swirl, a dance divine,
A little caffeine, and I'm feeling fine.
With every splash, laughter reigns,
A simple sip eases my pains.

Pour me another, let's dream big,
Overflows and joy, it's not so vague.
In the rhythm of life, there's a score,
Cheers to the mornings and the power of a pour!

Navigating the Nebula

In the kitchen, stars collide,
Pots and pans on this joyride.
Coffee cosmos, swirling bright,
Seeking meaning in each bite.

Spilling dreams like stardust fine,
With each sip, the world's a line.
Floating through a galaxy warm,
Caffeine's power, a perfect charm.

Chaos reigns like meteors fly,
I sip my brew, watch dreams go by.
Navigating troubles, bright-eyed flight,
Finding purpose in each delight.

So raise your mug to the cosmic grind,
In this universe, joy's well-defined.
With every pour, I chart my way,
In the nebula of life, I play.

Awakening the Soul

A mug in hand, I greet the morn,
My dreams are brewed, my patience worn.
I seek the light, but where's my cup?
The world spins slow, so fill it up!

With every sip, the fog will clear,
A jolt of joy, a burst of cheer.
I muse on life, and what it means,
While jangling keys and chasing beans!

Brewed Ambitions

I rise from bed with sleepy eyes,
My plans are lofty, but so are pies.
A coffee drip, a rich delight,
To fuel my dreams that soar in flight.

Espresso shots, my secret fuel,
I plot my course, I'm no one's fool.
Yet here I sit, just one more sip,
To chase my goals, a daring trip!

The Quest for Meaning

Oh, where's the truth in frothy cream?
I ponder life's great coffee dream.
A cup in hand, I seek the wise,
But find just bubbles in the guise.

Is meaning found in coffee grounds?
Or in the lore that laughter sounds?
I swirl my drink, a daring mix,
And wonder how to mend the fix!

Sip of Clarity

A sip, a gulp, a joyful cheer,
My mind's a haze, but oh so clear!
With every drop, the answers flow,
To questions I've yet to bestow.

In caffeine dreams, my thoughts collide,
With zany tales that won't subside.
A cuppa joy, my potion bright,
I laugh and sip, my future's light!

Rich Aromas of Existence

Waking up with dreams so bold,
Heart desires a story told.
Brewed ambitions fill the air,
Coffee mug, my secret flair.

Each sip a chance to redefine,
Chasing life and caffeine's line.
With frothy milk and laughter's cheer,
I sip my doubts, make them disappear.

Beans of wisdom ground so fine,
In a cup, life's little sign.
The aroma dances, whispers clear,
"Just take a gulp, the path is near!"

Stirring thoughts with cinnamon twist,
Not a chance I'll ever miss.
With every pour, I boldly strive,
In this mug, I feel alive!

Where Dark Waters Meet Light

Beneath the surface, flavors swirl,
Dark and bitter, a playful whirl.
Coffee waves crash on the shore,
In every cup, I seek for more.

Espresso dreams, a little strong,
No time for doubt, I'll hum a song.
Sipping slowly, tasting fate,
Every drop, I celebrate.

Creamy clouds flow over spills,
In this mug, ambition thrills.
Where shadows meet the morning bright,
I laugh and sip to my delight.

Chocolate whispers, sweet and bold,
Life's little secrets to be told.
In every brew, a journey tight,
Where dark waters meet the light.

Sipping from Life's Overflowing Mug

Life's a blend, so rich and deep,
Pour it over, taste and keep.
With a splash of joy and dash of fun,
I raise my cup—let's get it done!

Every morning, brew the dream,
Stir my worries in the steam.
The world awaits, let's take a ride,
With caffeine's boost, I feel alive!

Mugs overflowing, laughter spills,
Sipping wisdom, chasing thrills.
No bitter taste can dampen cheer,
In every sip, my path is clear.

So here's a toast to all the brews,
To every laugh and little muse.
In this rich cup, my spirit hugs,
Sipping joy from life's warm mugs.

The Barista of Destiny

In the café of life, I wait,
Order dreams, it's never late.
Beans of fate ground just for me,
Pouring visions, wild and free.

The barista smiles, a wink and brew,
"Today's special, just for you!"
He mixes in a pinch of grace,
With every sip, I find my place.

Lattes swirl with hints of hope,
Sipping slowly, I learn to cope.
With every cup, I taste the fun,
In this café, we've just begun.

So here's to life, a playful grind,
With every toast, our hearts aligned.
In the hands of fate, we find our plea,
The barista of destiny brews for me!

Awakening Ambition

I stumbled from my cozy bed,
My dreams still swirling in my head.
With tangled hair, I face the day,
And wonder what I'll brew today.

The fridge gives me a silent stare,
While I debate my morning fare.
Eggs or toast? A fruit delight?
Or just a donut, oh what a sight!

Outside the sun begins to shine,
But first, I need that mug divine.
The aroma wafts, it fills the air,
My sleepy self begins to care.

I laugh as caffeination's near,
With every sip, my fate grows clear.
Life's a puzzle, I'm the piece,
Fueled by coffee, I find my peace.

Steeped in Reflection

Sipping slowly, thoughts take flight,
A cup in hand, feels just right.
The steam rises, dreams emerge,
With every sip, ambitions surge.

What to be? A jester or sage?
Maybe a chef or a coffee wage?
The liquid magic warms my soul,
As I ponder my next bold role.

Pour another cup, let's explore!
Life is a brew, so much in store.
I stir my dreams, add some cream,
In this café of my wildest dream.

Each gulp a laugh, each drop a cheer,
With every sip, my path is clear.
To joke, to dance, to simply be,
All served up in a cup of glee.

Echoes of Energy

With every clink of porcelain bright,
I feel the buzz, the pure delight.
The clock ticks on, but I don't care,
This cup of joy is floating in air.

I take a gulp, my spirits soar,
Sending whispers, wanting more.
"Find yourself!" they teasingly say,
While I sip on this bright café.

Laughter bubbles up like foam,
In this mug, I feel at home.
Chasing thoughts like a wild breeze,
Filling my heart with sips of ease.

So I recline, enjoy the show,
Life is short—let laughter flow.
As echoes dance around the room,
I find my purpose in each plume.

Steaming Introspection

The pot gurgles a joyous tune,
As I debate the sun and moon.
Should I rise? Or should I rest?
With coffee's warmth, I feel the best.

Reflecting on my nine-to-five,
A quest for dreams, I must revive.
Should I write, or maybe paint?
Or just admire a coffee saint?

Steam curls up, clouds in my mind,
As I sip and seek to unwind.
Each moment slow, like honey's flow,
Brewing thoughts I want to grow.

So here I sit, mug embraced tight,
Chasing whims in morning light.
With laughter steeped in every drop,
This search for joy will never stop.

Reflections in a Coffee-Stained Cup

A splash of brown, a swirl of cream,
My thoughts float here, a caffeinated dream.
With every sip, I ponder my fate,
While all around me, the beans oscillate.

The barista grins, he knows my game,
Each morning ritual, it feels the same.
Yet in this mug, I seek delight,
A blend of chaos, morning's light.

Pursuing the Perfect Roast

I scour the shelves, my heart's aflame,
For that elusive, enchanting name.
Is it too dark? Or maybe too bright?
In this caffeine quest, I'll win the fight.

Espresso shots dance, they tease my brain,
With every drop, I feel the gain.
Yet someone's laughter, oh, such a jest,
Am I a coffee lover or just obsessed?

A Voyage in a Venti Cup

Each gulp a wave, I ride the froth,
Moments of bliss, I dare not sloth.
A lid that clinks, a journey begins,
Through caramel rivers, my spirit spins.

The world rushes by, but here I sit,
With dreams afloat, each sip is lit.
A personal cruise in a paper hull,
Caffeine dreams make my heart feel full.

Savoring Purpose, One Sip at a Time

In this cup, I find my muse,
With every sip, I'll refuse to lose.
A splash of joy, a dash of grit,
Whoa, this coffee's got some wit!

The clock ticks madly, my thoughts align,
Fueled by brew, I'll be just fine.
Each frothy sip, a leap of grace,
Pour me more, I'm in this race!

Awakening the Soul's Brew

Mornings stumble, eyes half-closed,
A quest begins, caffeine-hazed prose.
With each sip, thoughts take flight,
Dreams percolate, oh what a sight!

Jugs and mugs, a splendid parade,
Where ambitions brew, and fears will fade.
A frothy crown on a latte king,
Who knew beans could make the heart sing?

Spilling wisdom, one drop at a time,
The clock ticks loud, keeping perfect rhyme.
Each cup holds a secret glint,
No more snoozing, it's time to sprint!

Laughter bubbles with each sip's grace,
In this dance of din, I find my place.
A jester's brew, a muse's delight,
With coffee in hand, the world feels right!

The Quest for Meaning in Every Sip

The day begins with a steaming cup,
A muddy miracle, helps me get up.
I search for truths in every pour,
Why can't I find the meaning more?

Espresso shots and a playful grin,
Is it just caffeine or is it within?
I ponder my fate over milky foam,
With every sip, I feel more at home.

Coffee grounds and comedic clatter,
Who knew within lies between the chatter?
Mirth in a mug, giggles abound,
In this caffeinated chaos, joy's found!

So I swirl my troubles with sugar and cream,
Laughing as life drips into a dream.
The quest is messy, but oh, so divine,
With every sip, I know I'll be fine!

Fading Echoes of Morning Dreams

Morning whispers, dreams start to fade,
In sleepy mugs, my hopes are laid.
A java jolt, my mind awakes,
To chase those dreams, a road it takes.

Pour it strong, make the laughter flow,
As fragrant thoughts claim the morning glow.
The chase for meaning, a comic spree,
Each gulp a giggle, endless glee!

The sun peeks in, shadows retreat,
With every slurp, I tap my feet.
Conversations brewed with every drop,
In this caffeinated carnival, we hop!

In search of sense, I stumble and trip,
But coffee's warmth is my trusty grip.
With swirling mugs and overly sweet dreams,
There's laughter to spare, or so it seems!

A Journey Beyond the Steam

Steam curls up, a lively dance,
Guiding my thoughts in a caffeinated trance.
Each swirl a story, each sip a cheer,
The journey unfolds, never fear!

Sipping slowly, a giggle escapes,
Finding the joy in funny shapes.
What's brewed today? A riddle to find,
Adventure awaits in every grind.

Beans of wisdom, roasted with flair,
In this coffee shop, dreams fill the air.
With each chuckle, the depths I explore,
Fueling my laughter, I wander for more!

So raise your cup, join this ballet,
In the world of coffee, let's frolic and play.
Life's steamy essence pours like a stream,
In the warmth of the brew, I truly beam!

The Art of Brewing Belief

With cup in hand, I ponder life,
Each sip I take, smooth as a knife.
The steam curls up, a dreamy dance,
In caffeinated bliss, I find my chance.

But who am I in this frothy swirl?
Am I a barista or just a girl?
The grind begins, the beans collide,
And with each pour, my thoughts are wide.

Beyond the Beans: Seeking Significance

A latte art heart, a pyramid scheme,
Is this my purpose or just a dream?
Decaf dilemmas haunt my soul,
Can froth fulfill a life-long goal?

I spill the cream in wild dismay,
Is meaning lost in the café fray?
Each sip a giggle, each drip a grin,
Solving life's puzzles with a touch of gin.

Grounds for Reflection

The coffee grounds tell tales untold,
Secrets of mornings, both timid and bold.
I ponder deep while swirling my cup,
Finding true purpose, I won't give up.

With every pour-over, dreams take flight,
In the frothy abyss, I seek the light.
Grounds whisper wisdom as I abide,
Navigating life, with caffeine as my guide.

The Philosopher's Brew

Am I a thinker or just caffeine's fool?
Debating life's meaning inside this brew pool.
Complexity swirls in a mug so profound,
Coffee and queries, my thoughts are unbound.

Stirring up chaos, a dash of the absurd,
Every sip brings back memories stirred.
The philosopher's quest in a java-filled haze,
Finding my truths in the coffee's warm gaze.

The Brewed Experience

I wake up in a sleepy daze,
A cup of joy begins my phase.
I stumble through the morning grind,
To find that boost I hope to find.

The kettle sings a merry tune,
I dance around like a cartoon.
With steam that swirls and swishes by,
It lifts my spirit way up high.

Each sip a jolt, each gulp a cheer,
My coffee mug, the best frontier.
In caffeine dreams, I laugh and play,
Imbibing bliss to start my day.

So here's to brews both strong and bold,
With every cup, a story told.
In mugs of warmth, I chase the sun,
And brew my joys 'til day is done.

Brewing Bravery

With each drip from the pot, I ponder,
Am I brave enough to take this wander?
The bubbles pop, they seem to know,
Courage brews with every flow.

The first sip hits like a sunny ray,
Awakens dreams, come what may.
In a world of cups, I find my way,
My heart's delight begins to play.

A frothy art, a latte's song,
In this caffeinated world, I belong.
I conquer fears with every blend,
A brave new dawn, where flavors send.

So raise your mugs and let them shine,
In steaming cups, our hopes align.
For every brew spills joy anew,
In every sip, my courage grew.

Grounded in Grains

With beans so dark, my day begins,
In this ritual, my soul just grins.
I grind my way to morning's bliss,
Each crack and pop, not one I miss.

A splash of cream, a sprinkle sweet,
This frothy magic can't be beat.
The grains, they ground my tangled mind,
In coffee's warmth, my peace I find.

As swirling swirls of caramel sway,
I giggle at my silly ballet.
With every cup, laughter beans the way,
I caffeinate my silly play.

So here's to grains that lift us high,
In cups of joy, we touch the sky.
Each sip a journey, bold and grand,
In every pour, I take a stand.

Seeking Serenity in Steam

In clouds of steam, I find my calm,
A gentle waft, a soothing balm.
I close my eyes, take a deep breath,
In coffee's embrace, I flirt with death.

The world outside may spin and race,
But in this mug, I've found my place.
With every swirl, I let things be,
Serenity in every cup I see.

A dance of flavors, sweet and bright,
I sip my brew, embrace the light.
In chaos, I seek my cozy nook,
A pause to breathe, a warming book.

So raise a cup to steaming dreams,
In playful sips, reality gleams.
With laughter bubbling, days seem supreme,
In every froth, we chase our dream.

A Cup Half Full

In a world of beans and brews,
I ponder life while sipping stews.
Between the sips of my café delight,
I search for meaning in the morning light.

The barista winks, I flash a grin,
A frothy latte, where do I begin?
With every drip, I start to muse,
Is it the coffee, or the news I choose?

With cream and sugar, my thoughts unwind,
What's the purpose? Let's not be blind!
I slurp, I sip, and giggle with glee,
Is my life a joke? But hey, there's caffeine!

So here I sit with mug in hand,
Finding reason in a rich coffee land.
With every taste, my doubts dissolve,
In this cup half full, I start to evolve.

The Aroma of Aspiration

Morning awakens with a brewed embrace,
A whiff of hope in this cozy space.
Beans are grinding, a hopeful sound,
In each fragrant swirl, new dreams abound.

I sip and ponder, is that my fate?
Should I stir in wisdom, or just sugar plate?
With flavored hopes and dreams aglow,
Each cup I craft, more zest to show.

The espresso shot, a tiny thrill,
In this mug, I seek to fulfill.
With laughter steeped in rich ambitions,
Do I chase a dream, or change traditions?

So here I toast, to each bold blend,
In this café life, may joy not end.
With mugs raised high, let purpose flow,
In the aroma of dreams, let's steal the show.

Wandering While Waking

I roam through kitchens, seeking a find,
A cup of magic, brewed for the mind.
With grumbles and groans of morning's start,
I wander aimlessly, caffeine my art.

A journey awaits, on foot or in dreams,
To coffee shops bursting at the seams.
With every step and hopeful glance,
What's my calling? Should I take a chance?

Each sip ignites a giggle or cheer,
A path of flavor, it's very clear!
With steam and froth, I take my quest,
To find my rhythm, my ultimate jest.

So here I dance through drowsy haze,
In search of joy in the morning blaze.
Each sip a step, each laugh a call,
Wandering while waking, I'll have it all!

Find Your Blend

In this world of beans both bold and bright,
I seek the blend that feels just right.
With a splash of whimsy and a dash of fun,
In every cup, let my journey be spun.

I try the flavors, each sip a test,
A mocha whirl, an espresso quest.
With frothy clouds and milky waves,
I giggle at my caffeinated braves.

The barista laughs, I give a wink,
What do I mix? More sugar, I think!
With laughter brewed and dreams on the side,
In this swirl of taste, watch my hopes glide.

So grab your cup, let's raise it high,
In this funny quest, let's touch the sky.
For in every blend, there's magic to send,
Let's sip together, and with laughter, mend!

Dreaming with a Drip

Woke up with a heavy head,
The world feels like a foggy dream.
Chasing thoughts that dance and spread,
All I need is liquid steam.

Pour it slow, don't rush the flow,
This brown elixir brings a grin.
With every sip, my worries go,
Let the caffeine tide begin.

Stirring hopes in mug so wide,
I plot my day with frothy art.
Beneath the layers, dreams reside,
Oh, sweet brew, you warm my heart.

Time to laugh and lose my doubt,
With each cup, I find my way.
Life should not be all about,
But the joy of every play.

Mocha Musings

Sipping slowly, thoughts collide,
A swirl of chocolate, cream, and joy.
I ponder life, with mocha as my guide,
This frothy cup's my favorite toy.

Dreams on the table, just like stray beans,
They bounce around, never too tame.
With every gulp, absurdity leans,
As I sip my sweetened game.

Why do folks rush through the grind?
I'll take my time, thank you very much.
With whipped cream peaks, clarity I find,
An espresso shot? Just a crutch.

The day may come and pass me by,
But I'll savor each pour that I meet.
In cups of joy, I'll freely fly,
With chocolate dreams, my life's sweet treat.

The Brewed Journey

Maps of beans spread on the floor,
Adventures bubble in every cup.
I try to taste what's brewed before,
As laughter rises and sips erupt.

From the dark roast to shining gold,
I measure life by caffeine's flow.
Tales of travels, ages unfold,
In every pour, new friends I know.

Stirring stories with a spoon,
I search for meaning in my blend.
Each catchphrase brewed under the moon,
Life's bitter grind can truly mend.

So raise a mug to whims and dreams,
A journey painted brown and warm.
From playful sips to coffee themes,
In every laugh, a new norm.

Espresso of Existence

A shot of dark, a shot of fun,
Life's too short for lukewarm brew.
I sip and giggle, work undone,
Feeling free, with much to do.

The aroma lifts my weary frame,
In this mug, the world stands still.
Caffeine kicks, ignites the flame,
A cosmic blend, my heart to fill.

So here I am, a smile wide,
With every cup, I find my beat.
Life's quirky curves become my ride,
In espresso shots, my heart's retreat.

Don't fret the grind, just let it pass,
Find joy in every darkened space.
In steaming cups, sweet moments last,
With laughter, coffee's warm embrace.

Sips of the Soul

Each morning, I brew a cup,
A jolt to wake my sleepy gut.
With every sip, I ponder life,
Should I bake, or just avoid strife?

The coffee whispers, 'Rise and shine!'
But snooze commands, 'You're still divine!'
A battle rages in my brain,
One sip in, I'll dance in the rain.

Mugs piled high like stacked-up dreams,
The caffeine flows, ignites my schemes.
In the steam, my thoughts collide,
Drink up, friend, it's time for a ride!

So here I sit, with cup in hand,
Trying to figure out life's plan.
When beans' aroma fills the air,
I find my purpose in a chair.

Rituals of Reflection

At dawn, my kitchen sings to me,
A ballet of smells, a fragrant spree.
I dance with beans, the grind so sweet,
Life's riddle hides beneath my feet.

With each pour-over, thoughts combine,
Brewed liquid wisdom, so fine, so divine.
Stir the cream, the sugar, too,
Is clarity near, or am I just blue?

Swirling thoughts in my favorite mug,
Do I chase dreams or just get snug?
I sip with glee, the chaos slows,
Never underestimate what coffee knows.

In this ritual, I find my peace,
With every gulp, my tensions cease.
Coffee's warmth holds secrets tight,
In cups of comfort, I seek the light.

Riding the Ripple

A splash of cream, a twist of fate,
Frothy clouds dance, oh, isn't it great?
I take a sip, and then a ride,
On caffeine waves, let worries slide.

My mind's a tangle, thoughts a maze,
Yet coffee's bliss leads through the haze.
I gallop forth, on joy's sweet tide,
With every cup, my hopes collide.

I fetch a refill, with giddy zeal,
Dashing through dreams, oh, what a meal!
Scrambled ideas, that's how it goes,
On this bean breeze, anything blows!

So join the ride, don't miss the show,
It's a whirlwind quest on a coffee flow.
When you sip and laugh, oh what a thrill,
Life's spicy brew gives hearts a fill.

Grounds for Growth

In the pot, grounds swirl and spin,
A dance of life, where dreams begin.
Late-night brews and morning jests,
One cup more, that's where life tests.

With each rich sip, I ponder fate,
Is this the day, or just too late?
The mug is full, my heart is light,
I'll figure things out, it'll be alright.

The grounds reveal their hidden truths,
In swirls of dark, the answer soothes.
A little splash, a dash of grace,
In coffee's depths, I find my place.

So raise your cup, let worries go,
With every gulp, possibilities grow.
In laughter, love, and steaming brews,
We chase the dreams that we can choose.

The Caffeine Chronicles

I wake up in a daze, feeling quite absurd,
My brain's a sleepy monster, it doesn't say a word.
I stumble to the kitchen, where the magic brews,
A cup could solve my problems, or at least diffuse.

The kettle starts to whistle, a symphony of dreams,
I dance like a caffeine fairy, bursting at the seams.
Pour the steaming potion, feel it warm my hands,
Suddenly I'm ready—come on, world, make plans!

Each sip's a little giggle, a jolt of pure delight,
As life becomes a circus, everything feels right.
The half-empty mug speaks wisdom, its surface gleams with cheer,
For all you need is coffee when the day's unclear.

So here's to all the dreamers, let's raise our mugs up high,

With every cup of liquid joy, our spirits start to fly.
In cups of roasted wonder, we'll find our silly way,
Now let's caffeinate the chaos, and laugh the day away!

Coffee-stained Paper

A paper lying idle, awaits a stroke of muse,
But first, a sip of magic, to shake the morning blues.
With dribbles and with droplets, the pages start to mark,
Each swirl a revelation, how inspiration sparks.

I spill my doubts in coffee, they swirl in dark delight,
My cover letter's ruined—oh, what a funny sight!
But every stain's a story, a history that's mine,
Each ring of mocha laughter, a tale that's truly fine.

I write my dreams in puddles, with splashes, drips, and stains,
The ink plays tag with java, as creativity reigns.
There's nothing quite so silly, as when the muse runs dry,

But with a cup of purpose, I can still give it a try.

So here's my ode to coffee, and all its charming mess,
In every sip, a giggle, in every drip, finesse.
May all my pages flourish, with mocha shades so bright,
For in this dance of caffeine, the chaos feels just right!

The Pursuit of Taste

In the morning's golden glow, my taste buds start to yearn,
For flavors bold and daring, it's now my time to learn.
I chase the sweet aroma, through countless café doors,
Each cup a tiny treasure, each sip opens new shores.

A caramel macchiato, with a frothy cloud on top,
Then there's the latte art, oh watch those hearts just pop!
But sometimes I get lost, in a mocha maze of cream,
A chocolatey adventure that makes my taste buds scream.

The search can be quite silly, as I swirl and slurp with flair,
Each sip a little riddle, bringing joy beyond compare.
Latex-free cappuccinos and chai that makes me dance,
With every cup, I wonder, do I stand a chance?

So let's laugh through the flavors, explore what each bean brings,
In the pursuit of this alchemy, where laughter surely sings.

For every sip a giggle, each blend a joyful toast,
In the world of tasty wonders, my love is what I boast!

Clarity in the Cup

There's clarity in coffee, in every steamy brew,
As I ponder life's great questions, and sip it through and through.
With frothy waves of wisdom, each swirl makes me believe,
That every cup's a teacher, if we just take a cleave.

The morning fog might linger, but caffeine cuts it sharp,
Like a comedian with punchlines, it strums a vibrant harp.

I raise my cup of magic, toast the day ahead,
In a mugs' bubble kingdom, where giggles can't be shed.

It tickles my imagination, with each delightful sip,
Making every ordinary moment feel like a comic strip.
"Why wear my serious face?" I chuckle, take a taste,
In this cup of clarity, silliness cannot waste.

So let's dance with the flavors, and mingle with the steam,

For clarity is fleeting, but humor's always deemed.
With coffee as my sidekick, I'll conquer every plight,
In this joyful little journey, a caffeinated flight!

A Journey, One Sip at a Time

With every cup, I ponder fate,
Is this caffeine or just a date?
The froth, it dances on my lip,
As I embark on my morning trip.

Each sip a step, each gulp a leap,
Through realms where dreams and brew do creep.
It spills, it splashes, makes a mess,
But oh, this ritual's pure success!

I meet my goals with every pour,
Where dreams erupt like coffee's roar.
The journey's wild, yet smooth and fun,
As I sip and sip until it's done!

In cups both big and some quite small,
I rise and shine, then start to stall.
But with each brew, I feel alive,
A journey where my dreams can thrive.

Wakeful Whispers

The sun peeks in, it's way too bright,
My coffee's here to save the night.
With whispers sweet and blissful steam,
I search for sense, or so I dream.

"Hey you!" it says, "Don't go back to bed!"
"Your thoughts are waiting, come be fed!"
A swirl of cream, a dash of fun,
Awake I am, and now I run!

I spill my plans with frothy grace,
While in the mug, ideas race.
With every sip, new plans ignite,
A laugh, a smile, feels just so right.

Oh, what a thrill, this dance of taste,
In every cup, no time to waste.
So steer your dreams with stirring cheer,
And let your coffee steer you near!

Grounds of Discovery

In tiny beans, great truths are found,
With every grind, wisdom's unbound.
A ritual steeped in playful tease,
What secrets lie beneath the freeze?

Each darkened cup a roadmap spun,
To lands of laughter, oh what fun!
I ponder, sip, explore my mind,
As coffee grounds help me unwind.

A sprinkle here, a splash of that,
What else can brew inside this hat?
The chalky bits of past success,
Turned to flavor, I must confess!

So here I sit, a wise old bard,
My coffee mug a trusty guard.
For in the grounds, I find my way,
And chuckle at the mess of day!

The Bean's Odyssey

From plant to cup, what a long ride,
I search for answers, full of pride.
With every bean a tale to tell,
Of sleepy mornings, they break the spell.

A grind of joy, a splash of flair,
The odyssey, not a single care.
With each new brew, a world unturned,
In stories rich, my mind has churned.

I journey far on caffeine's wings,
Tasting life, what laughter brings!
With coffee's caper taking flight,
My purpose brewed till late at night.

So join me now, let's sip away,
With playful beans, we start the day.
Adventure calls through every mug,
In this great quest, where dreams can hug!

The Journey of a Wandering Heart

A heart that roams through streets unkempt,
In quests for warmth, the soul exempt.
With every sip, a laugh unfolds,
As stories brewed like tales retold.

Each cup a sign, a clue, a guide,
Through twists and quirks the dreams abide.
The map a swirl on porcelain white,
Directions lost in morning light.

Adventures rise, the froth anew,
With each espresso, what's the view?
I wander wide, yet her I chase,
With coffee charms and a goofy grace.

The final sip, a hopeful cheer,
For every cup, I hold more dear.
A journey shared, a taste divine,
My heart may roam, but oh, that line!

Espresso Dreams

In a café nook, I sip my fate,
With wonders brewed, I contemplate.
The barista winks, a knowing smile,
I ponder life in coffee style.

A double shot of comic relief,
With frothy mounds, I dance with grief.
The cream runs wild, my thoughts are thick,
Espresso dreams, I'll pick, I'll pick.

My cup it spills, a minor mess,
A world transformed in coffee's press.
With every drop, I laugh and sigh,
In search of dreams, I sip and fly.

The final froth, a blissful fate,
In steamy cups, I celebrate.
Each gulp a giggle, joy's sweet theme,
In caffeine's grip, I live the dream!

Mornings of Reflection

Awake at dawn, the pot does hum,
A symphony for morning fun.
With sleepy eyes, I pour with grace,
A ritual hug of warm embrace.

I jog my thoughts with sips of brew,
Like morning jogs—just me and you.
Between each gulp, the world's a blur,
Reflecting on why things occur.

The mug a throne for rambling minds,
In every creak, new wisdom finds.
A buttery croissant warms my soul,
Yet laughter leads—both light and whole.

As steam dances, my thoughts take flight,
In morning's glow, I find delight.
Each swirl brings cheer, a playful tease,
In caffeinated grace, I seize the ease!

Caffeine and Contemplation

In corners dark where shadows play,
I sip my thoughts, a mug to sway.
Each gulp a ponder, deep and loud,
In caffeine's grasp, I feel so proud.

The world's a joke, a cozy quip,
With every drink, I let it rip.
A latte swirl, a mocha muse,
Life's silly paths, I love to choose.

Conversations brewed in swirling steam,
With friends and laughs, we share the dream.
A shot of joy, or maybe two,
In cups of warmth, we find what's true.

As caffeine flows, the thoughts align,
In every sip, I'm feeling fine.
With laughs and clinks, we toast with glee,
In coffee's arms, we're wild and free!

The Waking Wanderlust

With dreams of grandeur, I awake,
Coffee cups, the deals we make.
Life's baffling puzzle, oh what a mess,
Chasing goals, but first, a blessed espresso.

Through tangled thoughts, I weave and roam,
In cafes bright, I find my home.
Add milk, sugar, a spritz of glee,
For every sip, my soul is free.

The quest for meaning, a quirky game,
While pondering why I got on this train.
But lo! There's comfort in every brew,
A latte speaks louder than wisdom too.

So, with each gulp, I dance and sway,
Finding joy in the sips I play.
Ambitions brewed in a dark roast mug,
Life's caffeine rush, a warm, snug hug.

Coffeehouse Conversations

In a nook, beneath bright neon lights,
Friends gather round for late-night rites.
With mugs in hand, we spill our dreams,
And argue over who's spilled their beans.

Ideas froth like a cappuccino's foam,
We dissect life like it's a tome.
The barista grins, pouring tales anew,
While we sip the chaos of me and you.

Laughter echoes, the topics roam,
From wild ambitions to finding a home.
Our banter brews, rich and loud,
In this caffeine-fueled, dreamer's crowd.

As we sip and slide into midnight talks,
Philosophy poured with extra frocks.
In this coffee haze, clarity comes,
In cups we trust, our minds like drums.

Aroma of Ambitions

The scent of dreams wafts through the air,
A brewing promise, beyond compare.
With every pour, a feature unfolds,
Chasing aspirations, in tones bold.

In the morning light, I brew my fate,
A rich dark roast, let's not wait.
I stir in goals with a dash of cream,
Chasing whims, life feels like a dream.

Oh, the adventures that beans can bring,
A sip of courage, I'm ready to spring.
In each warm cup, a story is told,
Bold ambitions, both brash and gold.

So raise your mugs, let's drink to the day,
With a chuckle and grin, we'll find our way.
The brew is brewing, oh what a tease,
In caffeine's theatre, I'll do as I please.

The Elixir of Exploration

A steaming cup, a path unclear,
With every sip, I shed my fear.
Exploring life one drink at a time,
Espresso shots feel like a rhyme.

In coffee shops, the world feels grand,
Adventures brewing, like grains of sand.
With a sprinkle of laughter, I travel far,
In a latte's warmth, I find my star.

The daily grind, yet joyfully spent,
In search of meaning, wherever I went.
Sipped with laughter, oh what a brew,
Each moment savored, life feels anew.

So here's to cups filled to their brim,
To dreams we chase and chances slim.
In the aroma of beans, I find my way,
With humor and coffee, I'll seize the day.

Quest for the Elusive Brew

I wander the streets, both far and wide,
With dreams of a cup, I cannot hide.
The scent of the grind, it leads me on,
To caffeinated wonders, from dusk to dawn.

A line at the shop, oh what a wait,
Lost in my thoughts of the perfect plate.
A sip of that dream, the golden elixir,
I might just find joy, each sip a fixer.

But spills on my shirt, oh what a scene,
From sloshing the brew, I'm less than clean.
A giggle erupts, the laughter unfolds,
As I navigate life, with stories retold.

Each cup tells a tale, a twist or a turn,
In every warm gulp, new lessons I learn.
So onward I go, fill my mug to the brim,
With laughter and joy, my purpose is whim.

Rise and Roam

The rooster crows loud, but I snooze just a bit,
My love for the bean keeps me in this split.
With dreams of a latte and foam stacked high,
I rise from the sheets, but my heart's still shy.

Adventuring out, I stumble and trip,
But coffee's the treasure, my reason to zip.
A drive-through delight, oh that glorious blend,
A friend for the journey, a sip to transcend.

The world is a circus, with mugs in the air,
I take every gulp like I've climbed Everest stairs.
With each funny sip, a chuckle ignites,
To find joy in each gulp, oh what a delight!

So here's to the journey, the coffee-fueled spree,
To laughter and moments that set my heart free.
Each caffeine adventure, a whimsical ride,
In search of my bliss, I cannot hide.

The Flavor of Fulfillment

In a world full of beans, I seek my delight,
With a splash of the cream, I'm ready to fight.
A mocha surprise or a bold dark roast,
The flavor of life, I simply can't boast.

I swirl in my cup, like a dance on a wire,
With steam in the air, I'm feeling inspired.
I spill on my pants, but who really cares?
Each drop is a gem, it's love in the layers.

Coffee's my muse, I'll sip and I'll sing,
With laughter surrounding, oh the joy it can bring.
I ponder my dreams with a frothy embrace,
In each little bubble, I find my own space.

So pour me a shot, let the fun never cease,
In search of a smile, let the brew grant me peace.
With humor and coffee, life's puzzle gets clear,
I cherish each moment, with laughter and cheer.

From Beans to Belief

I wake in a whirl, the beans on my mind,
In the quest for my brew, my purpose I find.
My grind is a journey, my heart is the key,
To sip and to savor, the best cup of glee.

A dapper barista, a wink and a grin,
Crafts magic from grounds, let the fun begin.
A sprinkle of sugar, a dash of pure cream,
With each little sip, I float on a dream.

But too much caffeine? Oh, don't call that bluff!
As I giggle and jitter, my antics get tough.
Leaping with energy, I burst into song,
Finding joy in the moments, the sweet and the wrong.

So here's to the chase, both silly and smart,
In mugs full of laughter, I find my true heart.
From beans to my soul, I create my own creed,
With coffee's embrace, my spirit is freed.

The Blend of Life

Morning fog in my head,
Like a brew gone quite wrong.
I sip the cup, feel alive,
But the taste is all gone.

Quests for meaning abound,
Like finding cream in the dark.
I ponder and sip, all the while,
Wondering where to embark.

With each caffeine-filled gulp,
I chase a fleeting thought.
Perhaps my purpose is here,
In the tumbler I've sought.

Yet, the froth keeps on swirling,
Just like my endless quest.
As I raise my cup high,
I toast to this messy jest.

Serving Purpose

Barista smiles, pouring dreams,
Steamy mugs of delight.
I ask her for wisdom,
She says, "It's all in the bite."

Scrambled thoughts in my mind,
Like sugar lost in the brew.
Am I just sipping away,
Or stirring life anew?

I flip through my planner,
In search of the grand scheme.
All I find are sticky notes,
And sketches of a dream.

Each latte a little nudge,
Towards the path I might take.
Maybe my purpose is here,
In the warmth of the wake.

Café of Contemplation

In a café, time just stops,
With pastries tempting the mind.
I search for the great epiphany,
With each donut I find.

The barista with knowing eyes,
Says wisdom comes with a sip.
So I order a double shot,
And settle in for the trip.

Amongst the chatter and clinks,
I ponder and sip with flair.
Is purpose just a tall order,
Or brewed in that cup of care?

But as the minutes get painted,
With laughter and dreams unturned,
I realize this is the essence,
Of all the lessons I've learned.

Brewing Dreams

A cup half empty or full?
Depends on how I perceive.
As I lift it to my lips,
I can't help but believe.

Coffee grounds whisper secrets,
Of journeys yet to unfold.
With each caffeinated gulp,
New stories will be told.

I seek the froth of meaning,
In the dregs of each brew.
In that milky swirl, I wonder,
What on earth should I do?

So I sip and I ponder,
With a grin on my face.
Perhaps my fate is wrapped up,
In this café's warm embrace.

Whispers in the Café

In a corner booth, I sit and sigh,
The barista winks, but I just can't fly.
Cup in hand, dreams swirl like cream,
This café's aroma fuels my daydream.

Caffeine's a muse, oh what a tease,
A dash of sugar, now I'm at ease.
Chatting with strangers, we laugh and agree,
Searching for meaning, while sipping the tea.

The clock ticks slow, as I ponder life,
Should I embrace joy or just add more strife?
With every sip, wisdom seems near,
Or maybe it's just my fourth cup, I fear.

But laughter resonates, it fills the air,
In this coffee sanctuary, I find my flair.
So I'll raise my mug to a life unplanned,
For every drop spilled, there's a story at hand.

Brewing the Elixir of Intent

Water's boiling, thoughts are brewed,
Mug in hand, I'm somewhat crude.
Pouring filters as I plot,
What is my aim? I've quite forgot!

Froth on top, looks like a hat,
My brain feels like a sleepy cat.
Do I seek fame or peace of mind?
Does anyone know? I'd like to find.

The jazz plays soft, as I sip slow,
Ideas bounce like popcorn, whoa!
With every gulp, new plans arise,
Wouldn't it be grand to be truly wise?

But what's this chat? Philosophy's near,
Over lattes shared, I lose my fear.
So here I stay, in delightful haze,
Brewing my dreams in the coffee maze.

Espresso of Enlightenment

Dark and rich, this shot does gleam,
Today's the day! Or so I dream.
Quick sip leads to sudden insight,
Or just too much caffeine, I might ignite.

I scribble thoughts on napkin sheets,
But all I write are chocolate treats.
Baristas laugh, they know my game,
Dancing with foamed milk, it's all the same.

Philosophers gather, cups in tow,
Spouting wisdom, but where'd it go?
I nod along, pretend I know,
While planning lunch, it's quite a show.

As espresso shoots through my veins,
Lucky charms or stubborn chains?
I chase the day with caffeinated cheer,
Searching for meaning, stop buying beer!

The Heart's Cup: A Steamy Pursuit

Every sip's a riddle, a heartfelt chase,
In this little café, I have my place.
Cup after cup, I ponder and muse,
Should I find love, or just drink the blues?

Steam rises high, like hopes in the air,
Flirting with thoughts, they seem to care.
Do I want depth, or just a light roast?
Maybe a pastry? That's what I'll boast.

From lattes art to poetic spills,
Laughter surrounds like comfy frills.
They chat about dreams, about where to go,
While I contemplate if I'm even in the flow.

So here I brew in this steamy retreat,
Seeking life's answers, coffee so sweet.
With each stray thought, I laugh and sip,
In this search of the heart, I'm on a fun trip.

The Café Chronicles: Stories Unfold

A barista's grin, a warm embrace,
Steam rises high, like dreams we chase.
With every sip, a story brewed,
In this cozy spot, our hearts are glued.

Croissants and jokes, a perfect blend,
The laughter's rich, it never ends.
Mugs clink like bells, a morning cheer,
In this haven, worries disappear.

A swirl of foam, art on display,
The caffeine rush, keeps sleep at bay.
Ideas float like sugar in cream,
Here's to madness, and all that we dream!

So grab a cup, let's spin our tales,
Life served hot, with all its trails.
Each drop a giggle, every sip a grin,
In this café life, we all win!

Mugs of Wisdom in the Quiet Hours

A gentle sip, the world slows down,
Mugs in hand, we lose our frown.
Conversations dance in the gentle hum,
While outside rages, the chaos drum.

Wisdom brewed with a hint of cream,
In quiet hours, we plot and scheme.
Thoughts rise like steam from the pot,
Finding meaning in every hot shot.

Laughter echoes, spills on the floor,
The perfect blend of lore and more.
With every cup, a new insight,
As day turns dusk, coffee fuels the night.

So raise your mugs to this sacred space,
Where time stands still, at our own pace.
The richest tales in each embrace,
Café wisdom, our saving grace!

Steeping in Serendipity

A twist of fate in a coffee shop,
Where strangers meet and laughter pops.
A spill of beans, a dash of chance,
In every sip, a joyful dance.

Sugar cubes like tiny dreams,
Whisking away the morning seams.
With every taste, unexpected glee,
Serendipity in a cup, you see.

Join the brew of whimsy and wonder,
Each moment shared pulls us from under.
Life's essence lingers at the brim,
We find our joy, even when it's slim.

So let's steep deep in this lovely brew,
Where surprises hide with every view.
In laughter and warmth, we will reside,
In this café corner, side by side!

Caffeine Dreams and Cosmic Themes

Under the stars, we gather tight,
With mugs in hand, we own the night.
Caffeine fuels our cosmic schemes,
On this adventure, nothing's as it seems.

The universe spills in every cup,
As we ponder why we wake up.
Dreams take flight like milk froth swirls,
In this brewhouse, life unfurls.

Galactic chatter, laughter so loud,
Fueling our hopes, making us proud.
Each sip a star, each grin a sun,
In this bizarre realm, we come undone.

So let's raise our mugs to cosmic fates,
In caffeine-soaked nights, let's tempt the plates.
Wander the universe, serene and free,
With dreams that drip like coffee, you see!

www.ingramcontent.com/pod-product-compliance
Lightning Source LLC
Chambersburg PA
CBHW071848160426
43209CB00003B/462